MASTER TODOIST

How to Use a Simple App to Create Actionable To-Do Lists

S.J. SCOTT

ISBN-13: 978-1-946159-04-5

Disclaimer

No part of this publication may be reproduced or transmitted in any form or by any means, mechanical or electronic, including photocopying or recording, or by any information storage and retrieval system, or transmitted by email without permission in writing from the publisher.

While all attempts have been made to verify the information provided in this publication, neither the author nor the publisher assumes any responsibility for errors, omissions, or contrary interpretations of the subject matter herein.

This book is for entertainment purposes only. The views expressed are those of the author alone, and should not be taken as expert instruction or commands. The reader is responsible for his or her own actions.

Adherence to all applicable laws and regulations, including international, federal, state, and local governing professional licensing, business practices, advertising, and all other aspects of doing business in the US, Canada, or any other jurisdiction is the sole responsibility of the purchaser or reader.

Neither the author nor the publisher assumes any responsibility or liability whatsoever on the behalf of the purchaser or reader of these materials.

Any perceived slight of any individual or organization is purely unintentional.

Contents

Your Free Gift

As a way of saying thanks for your purchase, I'm offering a free report that's exclusive to readers of *Master Todoist*.

With the *Master Todoist Companion Website*, you'll discover a series of walkthrough videos, all the screenshots included in this book and a quick reference guide for every link that I've mentioned. Everything you need to get started with habit stacking is included in the free companion website.

Go Here to Access the Master Todoist Companion Website

www.developgoodhabits.com/todoist-website

Join the DGH Community

Looking to build your goal-specific habits? If so, then check out the Develop Good Habits (DGH) community at **www.HabitsGroup.com**.

This is an excellent group full of like-minded individuals who focus on getting results with their lives. Here you can discover simple strategies for building powerful habits, find accountability partners, and ask questions about your struggles. If you want to "level up" the results from this book, then this is the place to be.

Just go to **www.HabitsGroup.com** to join the DGH Community.

Introduction

Why Todoist?

Feel overwhelmed by your daily tasks? Hate when you fail to make progress with your important projects? Want to manage your entire life with just one tool?

If you answered *yes* to any of these questions then you should consider incorporating the Todoist app into your life. Todoist is a program that's been around for over ten years. Millions of people use this app to:

- » create simple to-do lists and manage their tasks
- » build step-by-step project lists for their personal and professional lives
- » identify priority tasks that need to be completed immediately
- » create context-specific lists based on location, date, and energy levels
- » collaborate with team members on important projects
- » capture ideas and information that might be relevant in the future

In my opinion, Todoist is the perfect tool for managing *all* your day-to-day tasks. It has a simple design that allows you to start using it within the first five minutes of downloading it. But it's flexible enough to manage sophisticated projects that involve numerous steps and multiple team members.

At its core, Todoist is a task management application that helps to manage your personal and professional productivity. You can use it to manage your tasks from a smartphone, tablet, or computer. And it also has a premium version that enables collaboration with other members of your team.

Todoist was launched in January 2007 by Amir Salihefendic under the umbrella of the Doist company, which also offers a team communication tool called Twist.

The Todoist app is available in 17 languages:

1. Chinese (China)
2. Chinese (Taiwan)
3. Danish
4. Dutch
5. English
6. Finnish
7. French
8. German
9. Italian
10. Japanese
11. Korean
12. Norwegian
13. Polish
14. Portuguese
15. Russian
16. Spanish
17. Swedish

And it's available for these platforms and devices:

1. Web
2. Android Phone
3. Android Tablet
4. Android Wear
5. iPhone
6. iPad
7. Apple Watch
8. Windows
9. MacOS
10. Chrome
11. Firefox
12. Safari
13. Outlook
14. Gmail

Just go to any of the above sites online for the platform that you prefer then click (or tap) the download link to get started with the app.

Why I Recommend Todoist

The main reason you should consider this app is it's the perfect place to practice the "mind like water" concept that David Allen discusses in his book, *Getting Things Done*.

To quote Allen:

> *In karate, there is an image that's used to define the position of perfect readiness: "mind like water." Imagine throwing a pebble into a still pond. How does the water respond? The answer is, totally appropriately to the force and mass of the input; then it returns to calm. It doesn't overreact or underreact.*
>
> *The power in a karate punch comes from speed, not muscle; it comes from a focused "pop" at the end of the whip. It's why petite people can learn to break boards and bricks with their hands: it doesn't take calluses or brute strength, just the ability to generate a focused thrust with speed. But a tense muscle is a slow one. So the high levels of training in the martial arts teach and demand balance and relaxation as much as anything else. Clearing the mind and being flexible are key.*
>
> *Anything that causes you to overreact or underreact can control you, and often does. Responding inappropriately to your email, your staff, your projects, your unread magazines, your thoughts about what you need to do, your children, or your boss will lead to less effective results than you'd like. Most people give either more or less attention to things than they deserve, simply because they don't operate with a "mind like water."*

Allen's point is that your mind is the *worst place* to store your ideas, tasks, and appointments. Sure, you'll probably remember most things, but if you develop the practice of capturing every open loop in your life and putting them in one place, then you can free up your brain to focus on only the task right in front of you. And in my humble opinion, the best tool for doing all this is the Todoist app.

Now, I'll be the first to admit that there are many apps to help you manage tasks. Some of them are great! For instance, I've used (or heard positive things about) all the following apps:

» Trello

» Nozbe

» Remember the Milk

» Toodledo

» Any.do

» Wunderlist

The reason I prefer Todoist to the competition is due to its simple functionality. It's elegantly designed so that it's easy to figure out. Like you, I hate using any app that requires hours of education to learn. With Todoist, you can download it right now and create your first task list within five minutes.

On the other hand, Todoist has many advanced features that allow you to manage hundreds of tasks and projects—*without* making you feel overwhelmed.

I'm not saying that Todoist is necessarily better than any of the other apps I mentioned, but I have found that it's the most robust when it comes to managing all that you have to do every day. (We'll talk more about the specific benefits of Todoist in the next section.)

About Master Todoist

At this point, you might be asking yourself: "If Todoist is so simple to use, then why do I need to read a book about it?"

Well, the simplest answer is that, while Todoist isn't hard to understand, there are many cool features and strategies that many people fail to use. Furthermore, if you use Todoist incorrectly, this app can actually *hinder* your productivity.

Let me explain: Most to-do lists are a mix of reminders, appointments, tasks, and random goals. These can often cause you to feel overwhelmed. Even if you work diligently and complete dozens of tasks, you might end the day feeling frustrated because you didn't check off every item on your list.

The goal of *Master Todoist* is to help you **rethink** your to-do lists. On the surface, you'll find a walkthrough of all the app's features, but you'll also discover many strategies that can help you focus on the tasks that truly matter.

Specifically, you will learn how to:

» identify the activities that are most important for your personal and professional life

» remember every single date-specific appointment, meeting, and personal obligation

» create projects with clearly identifiable next steps

» use Todoist to remove the distractions and "noise" that prevent you from focusing on your big-picture activities

» implement the advanced features to streamline the most precious asset that you possess—your time

The trick to eliminating that feeling of overwhelm is to redesign the way you manage tasks. Todoist can help you do this. And in the following book, you'll learn how to maximize your results with this simple app.

About the Author

Before getting started, let me introduce myself and briefly talk about why I decided to write a book on Todoist.

My name is Steve "S.J." Scott. I run the blog Develop Good Habits, and I'm the author of a series of habit-related titles, all of which are available at HabitBooks.com.

The purpose of my content is to show how *continuous* habit development can lead to a better life. Instead of lecturing you, I provide simple strategies that are easy to use no matter how busy you get during the day.

As someone who is a recovering pen-and-paper, Post-It Notes for every task, kind of guy, I was drawn to Todoist because I was trying to simplify my life. After a bit of a learning curve, I now use it to manage *every* task and project in my life. In fact, I use Todoist so much that it's constantly open on all of my devices—i.e., my iPhone, tablet, and laptop computer.

At first, I downloaded Todoist to supplement my task management efforts with Evernote (another great app). But as I started to increasingly use Todoist, I found myself relying on this app more and more. Nowadays, I use this app to manage almost *every* aspect of my life: remembering appointments, building habits, working on complex projects, and creating reminders for important events.

I'd consider myself to be a Todoist "superfan." Heck, I've even achieved the Karma rank of Grand Master (I'll explain Karma in a bit.)

Through Todoist, I'm close to achieving a fully *paperless* work environment—except for the physical journal I use to take notes and explore my thoughts.

Todoist is one of my favorite apps. And, hopefully, by the time you finish *Master Todoist* (and implement what you've learned), you'll also love the app the way I do.

About the Screenshots and Links

Before we get started with the "meat" of this book, there is one thing I'd like to mention. While I've included many images in this book, there won't be a screenshot for every single feature that Todoist offers.

The reason is simple:

Todoist can be installed on 13 devices. This means it would be a *very* boring read (and a waste of your time) if I included screenshots and instructions for every single device. Instead, I recommend that you visit the Todoist page for your preferred platform and then spend a few minutes familiarizing yourself with how it works. You can do this by clicking the links below or visiting the Todoist home page and clicking on the appropriate icon in the list just below the banner.

1. Web

2. Android Phone

3. Android Tablet

4. Android Wear

5. iPhone

6. iPad

7. Apple Watch

8. Windows

9. MacOS

10. Chrome

11. Firefox

12. Safari

13. Outlook

14. Gmail

After installing Todoist, you'll discover a clear set of instructions that can show you how to get started with Todoist. In fact, before moving on, I recommend installing the app on *at least* one of your devices.

Seriously—go do it right now!

Another thing about the images: You'll probably notice that many of the screenshots will look different from what you see with your version of Todoist. Once again, that's because each of the 13 platforms has a unique layout. And, furthermore, Todoist is constantly updating and tweaking the app, so as we move into 2018 and beyond, the layout of Todoist will definitely change!

Finally, if you're someone who hates trying to view images on an e-reader screen or print book, then I recommend checking out the free companion website.

What you'll discover on this website is a series of videos and downloads that will walk you through the different features of Todoist. The information in these freebies will all be covered in this book, but sometimes it's easier to learn technology through a visual walkthrough instead of the written word. So I encourage you to check the companion website if you'd like to expand on what you're about to learn.

Well, I hope you're ready to master the Todoist app. Next we'll talk about the benefits of this app and why I think it's the best task management tool in the market.

8 Benefits of Using the Todoist App

After being introduced to Todoist, I have found that I can achieve a level of potential that I was never able to achieve before. Even my largest projects are made up of much smaller tasks, and Todoist helps me keep all my important information in one place. This allows me to live my life in a more organized manner, which ultimately leads to achieving my goals faster with more productivity.

On the other hand, if you're still on the fence about whether to try Todoist, then here are eight benefits that will hopefully convince you to make the switch.

#1. Todoist is available on ALL major platforms.

With Todoist's apps and extensions for all major platforms, your tasks will always be available to you. Whether you're on a desktop computer, on your laptop at the office, or on your phone or tablet, you will have constant access to the tasks that you need to complete.

What's more, if you're someone who likes wearable technology (like an Apple Watch), then you can review and add tasks directly through this device. No matter where you are or what you're doing, you will always have access to your list of tasks and projects in Todoist.

Now, you may not think that you always need access to information for your work projects. But what if you are out and need to check your calendar or identify a quick task that you can work on if you're waiting in line? Todoist allows you to have all of that at your fingertips, even if you are out running errands.

#2. Todoist uses push notifications that act as important reminders.

I usually turn off push notifications for any new app that I download. I find them to be intrusive and excessive, and they often pop up when I am trying to do something important.

However, the push notifications that are sent by Todoist are always relevant, and they can help you remember important tasks and appointments that you might otherwise forget. If you use reminders selectively (which I'll discuss later), these notifications will help you make sure you never miss a critical meeting or deadline.

#3. Todoist uses cloud storage to protect your tasks.

While I have found some other apps useful in the past when I was trying to keep myself organized, I would find very little benefit from that app if my tablet was at home with the app on it and I was somewhere else. When information is only stored on one device, it forces me to take that device everywhere I go.

With cloud storage, all the information that you put in Todoist can be accessed from any device. Cloud storage refers to a model where data is stored on remote servers that can be accessed from any Internet connection. The data is maintained, synced, operated, and managed by a cloud storage service provider.

Todoist's cloud storage will keep you from having to take your phone, laptop, and tablet with you everywhere you go. You can access this information even if you're on a new device—like a public computer in a library.

Additionally, if your device breaks or if you lose it, you can simply download the app on any new device and sign in to see that all your data is still available.

#4. Todoist offers an inexpensive premium version.

I have often found after using an app for a while that the premium version is necessary. However, with every company wanting to charge me a monthly or yearly fee for their services, I have to pick and choose which ones are really worth it. Using all of them really starts to add up quickly.

Not only is Todoist affordable, it's a steal for the benefits you receive. As of this writing, the app costs under $30 for the year, which is under $3 per month. For less than the cost of a cup of coffee, you can be completely organized and walk around with all the information you'll need at your fingertips.

We'll talk more about this premium version in the next section.

#5. Todoist is constantly updated.

In the past, I've used other apps to manage my tasks. These have been great for remembering shopping lists or a short list of tasks for the day. But while these have also been helpful, they'll often break when the developer stops working on the app or moves to another project. Once this happens, the app is essentially frozen in time and doesn't update with our constantly changing tech world.

With over 40 employees in 20 countries, Todoist is loyal to its 5 million users, which is also why many users choose to upgrade to the premium version. As users begin to see Todoist as a partner in their everyday lives, it becomes clear that this app is a long-term need for only a small investment.

With its growing membership, Todoist has the capital it needs to keep updating with new features, platforms, and languages. It won't become obsolete, forcing you to switch to new technology. It will always be applicable to the most updated technology. As technology evolves, Todoist will be right there beside us taking those same steps forward.

#6. Todoist has a distraction-free design.

Sure, I can appreciate all of the work that app developers put into adding bells and whistles to their products. But when it comes to accomplishing on my goals, I need to be laser-focused, not distracted by unnecessary buttons or pictures. Between social media, text messages, email, and in-person meetings, I don't need any more "noise" interrupting me when I am trying to accomplish my goals.

The distraction-free design of Todoist really shows me that the people behind the app want to put *my* project first, not theirs.

Unlike many other apps, it doesn't load up the screen with an excessive number of buttons, options, and other unnecessary things. Instead, when you open the app, all it presents are the exact tasks that you need to complete for the day. You have already put in the information you need to see, and that information is simply being relayed back to you.

This helps to simplify your to-do list and removes annoying distractions. With their clean design, Todoist only tells you what you need to know, not what they want you to know.

On the other hand, if you want to review your projects or plan your week, Todoist also designs the app so that it's easy to find this information with just a few taps or clicks. It's very easy to navigate and very user-friendly, no matter how much or how little you have stored on there. No matter what your tech background is, Todoist is intuitive.

#7. Todoist provides one central location for all your information.

Before I used Todoist, my productivity system was composed of a mixed bag of tools. Using a combination of weekly task sheets, habit apps, and multiple productivity programs, I often found things got left behind. Additionally, my information was often kept in different locations. While this can be good to keep distractions away, in this fluid world, sometimes I need to access something right away without a lot of searching.

Now I have one central location where I can store all my personal and professional obligations together, including my goals and habits.

Plus, there are some great hacks and tricks (which I'll discuss later) that you can use to sync up with other apps and software programs. For example, Todoist works well with programs such as Google Calendar, Slack, and Evernote. This allows me to schedule an activity with one of these other tools, and it will automatically show up on my list of tasks in Todoist.

It's a huge time-saver, knowing that I can rely on just one app to manage all the open loops in my life.

#8. Todoist allows for easy collaboration.

Often, I need to share my work with my virtual assistant or even people outside of my company. In my personal life, I need to share my shopping list with my wife in case she is going to the store without me. Being able to collaborate with other people is a really important part of being productive.

Todoist lets you easily share information with other people so they can be up to date as well. This is much more convenient than attaching links to emails or having to stop what you're doing to send a text message. You simply add and share on Todoist, and you can be confident that your recipient will have the information they need.

It really is that simple. Todoist helps people achieve their potential because it recognizes that everything we accomplish, no matter how big or small, is all about the steps that it takes to get there.

Having somewhere to store the necessary steps you take in life to be your best self is one of the most helpful tools you can have. Todoist can provide this to you in a current and relevant format without adding distractions to your life.

Should You Go Premium?

We've talked briefly about the premium version and how, unlike other productivity apps, it's surprisingly inexpensive. It's currently less than $30 per year for individual users and under $30 per user per year for teams. For less than $3 per month, you can access all the bonus features of the app that will skyrocket your efficiency and productivity.

So the question is: Should you upgrade to the premium version?

The answer depends on your personal situation. If you suspect you'll use the app daily, this expenditure is a no-brainer. On the other hand, if you don't commit to using it daily, paying for the premium version might be a waste of money.

I think it's a good investment because you'll unlock the following features when you upgrade to the premium version (which I'll explain throughout this book):

» task labels & reminders

» 200 active projects (increased from 80)

» 25 people per project (increased from 5)

» location-based notifications

» ability to add tasks via email

» task comments & file uploads

» automatic backups

» productivity tracking and charts

» iCal synchronization

» project templates

In my opinion, these bonus features are critical to managing your tasks efficiently—and they're offered at an extremely affordable price. That said, I do recommend trying the free version for a few days before subscribing to the premium features. If you find yourself using the app daily, then you should consider upgrading to the premium version because it will take your productivity to the next level.

Well, that about covers the preliminary information about Todoist. Now we'll talk about how to get started with the app, and then we'll dive into the core features that you'll use daily.

Getting Started with Todoist

Out of the box, Todoist doesn't look very fancy. After installing it, you'll see a screen that looks like this:

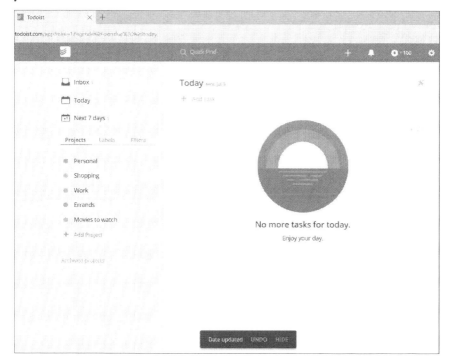

Sidenote: If you want to see a full version of this screenshot and the others mentioned in this book, then be sure to check them out on the free companion website.

At the top, you'll see your upcoming tasks and appointments. These are broken down into three options. All are self-explanatory:

1. **Inbox:** Think of this like the inbox of your email account. The tasks here are all the incompletes and open loops that you haven't

processed. You'll often use the Inbox when you want to add a task without having to add it to a specific project.

2. **Today:** These are the tasks that you've scheduled to be completed today (obviously). Typically, you'll spend the bulk of your time in this screen, working on the tasks that need to be processed immediately.

3. **Next 7 days:** This gives you a quick bird's-eye view of what's going on in the next week. You can use this to plan your week and pick the best days to work on specific tasks.

Below these three options are your project folders. The basic project list that Todoist offers is a mixed bag of personal and professional categories:

» Personal

» Shopping

» Working

» Errands

» Movies to Watch

Immediately to the right of the projects are two tabs: Labels **and** Filters, which we'll cover extensively later on.

Besides that, there aren't too many buttons on the basic screen of Todoist. And that's the beauty of this program. It's elegantly designed so you can hyper-focus on just the tasks that you need to complete. All the other features are kept out of sight until you need to access them.

For instance, at the top of the screen, you'll see a few buttons, like a plus sign, alarm bell, gear, and a circle.

If you click the gear symbol, you'll find a list of account features, which we'll cover next.

Account Features of Todoist

Todoist has many additional features that can help with your task management efforts. Some are interesting, but others (in my opinion) aren't critical to your success at completing your most important tasks.

To access these extra features, simply tap or click the gear symbol that's next to your account name to see the list of options. Here's how this would typically look in Todoist:

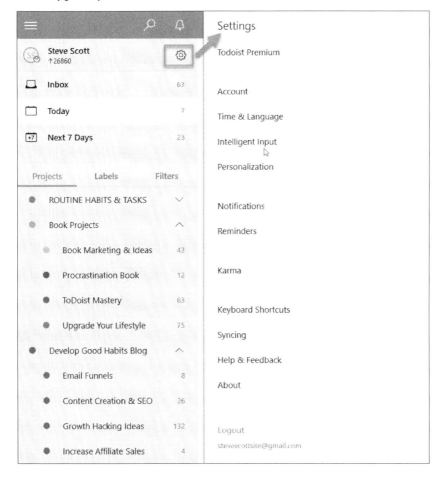

From there, you will see a series of options on this screen:

Account: This is used to edit or update your screen name and email address. It also gives you the address for your iCalendar Feed, which can be used to sync with other platforms. (We'll talk more about calendars in the next section.)

Time & Language: This feature lets you pick what day you'd consider to be the "start" of your week and designate the next weekday. Both options directly impact when a task will be scheduled when using the *Due Date* feature, which we'll cover in the next section.

The Time & Language feature can also be used to update your language preferences. But be *very* careful with this option because you don't to waste 30 minutes trying to figure out how to switch back to English when all you see are Chinese characters. (Like I did last month.)

Intelligent Input: This is part of the Smart Schedule feature by which Todoist can predict the best day for rescheduling tasks. While it's supposed to base these days on your previous activities, I have found that this feature doesn't work that well. Play around with it, but you might not find it to be very useful.

Personalization (or Theme): You can use this feature to customize your start page. Specifically, you can pick to display a project folder instead of today's tasks. This feature can also be used to change the color of the app—instead of the default red setting.

Notifications: Here you can select/deselect messages sent to your phone and/or email account for completing tasks, actions taken by collaborators, and comments mentioned to you. If you have team members who also use Todoist, then this feature provides a simple way to stay on top of what everyone else is doing.

Reminders: This feature can be used to set automatic reminders that will pop up for every task that needs to be completed at a certain time. You can choose from a few options:

- » 0 minutes before
- » 10 minutes before
- » 30 minutes before
- » 1 hour before
- » 2 hours before
- » no default reminder

If you're someone who needs reminders for those critical, time-sensitive tasks, then you can customize this feature to notify you whenever an important deadline is looming.

Keyboard Shortcuts: This feature can help you save time when using Todoist. Instead of having to tap or click certain options, you can choose from a series of shortcuts to add and edit your tasks.

Each platform has a different list of available shortcuts. So instead of boring you with a series of commands and characters, I recommend that you check out the Keyboard Shortcuts page that Todoist provides on their website.

Syncing: If you're like me, then you're someone who uses multiple devices for your work. So it's important that when you update or add a task on one device that it automatically shows up on all the other devices that have a Todoist account.

Unfortunately, sometimes your Todoist account won't automatically sync. So with this feature, you can tap or click this option to see when the app was last synced and to report any issues that you're currently experiencing.

Karma: Todoist uses Karma to "gamify" your productivity. Like any game, you can earn points for adding/completing tasks, keeping daily streaks, and achieving *Todoist Zero* (more about this later).

Basically, the more you use the app, the more points you'll earn. Furthermore, there are eight levels you can work up to as you gain points:

» Beginner—0 to 499

» Novice—500 to 2,499

» Intermediate—2,500 to 4,999

» Professional—5,000 to 7,499

» Expert—7,500 to 9,999

» Master—10,000 to 19,999

» Grandmaster—20,000 to 49,999

» Enlightened—50,000+

There are a few additional features that you'll find in the Karma screen:

» Create daily and weekly goals for the number of tasks you'd like to complete.

» Set the days of the week for when you're actively using Todoist.

» Toggle Karma to "On" or "Off".

» Set a "Vacation Mode" if you'd like to pause your Todoist activities.

» View tasks you've completed in total—over the last seven days, and over the last 4 weeks.

» View your daily and weekly streaks of completing your goals.

If you're someone who loves that sense of achievement when using an app, then Karma is a great tool for turning your to-do list into a fun experience.

That said, I believe it's better to focus on what's truly important than to obsess over checking dozens of tasks just to earn points. Feel free to use Karma, but also keep in mind that it's better to focus on the quality rather than quantity of your tasks.

Finally, I want to emphasize once again that some buttons and features in this tutorial might not match up to what you're seeing on your end. Just play around with the app and you'll probably find the feature hidden somewhere in Todoist.

Even though Todoist limits the number of features on the home screen, you still might not know where to get started with the app. That's why, starting in the next section, I will provide a feature-by-feature walkthrough of all that you can do with the app.

Before reading this section, I encourage you to fire up the Todoist app and follow along with the walkthrough that I'm about to provide. In my opinion, the best way to *learn anything* is to try things and play around with the different options.

Okay, now let's dive into the features. First up is the core Task screen, which forms the backbone of the app.

TASKS: The Core Feature of Todoist

Understanding the Tasks Screen

The bulk of your time in Todoist will be spent in the core Task screen. Whether you're adding items to projects like *Inbox, Today, Next 7 days*, or a specific project folder, your to-do lists are organized by the tasks that you decide to complete. So it's important to understand the function of the task screen and how it can help you manage your to-do lists.

To get started, simply select the **+ button** to add a task to your inbox or an existing project. Once this is selected, you'll see a screen like this:

The options you see on this screen help you to add important context to each task that you create. In a way, they answer the who, what, where, why, and how questions that you need to check off this item from your to-do list.

Here is a breakdown of how to customize each task:

"What do you want to get done?" or "Add a Task": Depending on what platform you're using, you'll see one of these questions, which acts as a prompt for adding a task.

This feature is self-explanatory—simply write down the specific task you'd like to complete.

Project: Select an existing project where you'd like to categorize this task. My recommendation is to put all your activities in a category that represents an important area of your life. We'll talk more about projects in the next section.

Label: Labels are great for adding context to a task. They could describe the location where it can be completed, or the total time it takes to do it, or the person/people involved with completing it, or if you're waiting for a specific item before you can take action on the task. Once again, this is a feature we'll explore in further detail later on in the book.

Priority: One great feature of Todoist is the ability to rank tasks in order of importance:

» Priority 1 (red flag): Most important

» Priority 2 (orange flag): Somewhat important

» Priority 3 (yellow flag): Slightly important

» Priority 4 (no flag): General tasks that need to get done, but aren't as important

Warning: At first, you might be tempted to mark multiple tasks with a red or orange flag because they all feel important. This is a mistake that I made. But if your tasks list is full of numerous priority 1 entries, you'll find it hard to identify the next action to work on.

It has been said that once upon a time, the word *priority* was used in the singular form, which meant you could only have one priority at a time. Unfortunately, in our modern frenetic world, everyone seems to have dozens of *priorities*.

In my opinion, if you'd like to truly master your time (and get the most from Todoist), you must be extremely selective about what you label as a priority. The only items that should get a priority 1 label are the tasks that absolutely, positively need to be completed by the end of the day.

To simplify things, whenever you're creating a task, you can type in a keyboard shortcode (or abbreviations) when creating task that represent these priorities. Like:

- » P1 for priority 1 tasks
- » P2 for priority 2 tasks
- » P3 for priority 3 tasks

Sure, these shortcode will only save you a few seconds, but when you create enough tasks in Todoist, these seconds really start to add up!

Add a Comment: Comments are used to add relevant information to this task, including multimedia files (i.e., images, audio, computer files, and even emojis) from your device.

Due Date: You can also add a date by which the task is completed. There are a number of options here.

First, you can pick a date on the calendar that pops up. Simply pick a day, and Todoist will assign it as a task for that day.

Next, you can use a number of shortcodes that let you add these **one-time tasks**. Here a few examples of words to type into Todoist that will automatically be recognized as a date-specific request.

> » *Today (or tod)*

> » *Tomorrow (or tom)*

> » *Today at 10:00 or Tomorrow at 10:00*

> » *Next week* (the default setting is Monday of next week)

» *Next month* (the default setting is the first day of the month)

» *Jun 1* (You can add an abbreviation for each month by entering the first three letters plus a number, then Todoist will recognize it as a specific day. So: Jan, Feb, Mar, Apr, May, Jun, Jul, Aug, Sep, Oct, Nov, or Dec.)

» *06/01/2017* (You can write out a numeric date by month, day, and year.)

» *8 p.m.* (You can type out a time and Todoist will schedule it for that day or for the next day if the time has already passed.)

» *7 hours* (Add a number, plus the word "hours" and you can schedule the completion of that task at that point.)

» *5 days* or *5 weeks* (Same concept. Type out a number and the word "days," Todoist will recognize it as something that should be scheduled at a later date.)

I know some of this might be confusing—it took me a while to get comfortable with all the shortcodes and abbreviations that Todoist uses. That's why I recommend getting started with the calendar feature to schedule tasks and then try the shortcodes when you're more familiar with the app.

Sidenote: You might get frustrated by the predictive nature of the shortcodes. Similar to the auto-correct feature on your phone, Todoist occasionally gets things wrong about the information you're trying to enter.

As an example, I have a weekly business meeting with my friend Tom. Unfortunately, whenever I type *Meeting with Tom,* Todoist thinks I mean, *Meeting with* (scheduled for tomorrow).

It's frustrating, to say the least. So I've had to change the wording to *Meeting with Thomas* in order for Todoist to let me add the full task.

You'll probably come across a few of these minor annoyances. But don't stress out if that happens. Simply create an adjusted name for the activity and then move on.

The final way to enter a due date is to schedule it as a *recurring* action. This is perfect for those habits and routines that you'd like to incorporate into your day.

It's easy to create a recurring task. Simply type the word *every*, followed by a number or day-specific description. Here are a few that you can include:

» Every day

» Every Monday (or any other day of the week)

» Every weekday (Monday through Friday)

» Every week (starts the day you add it)

» Every month (starts the day you add it)

» Every year (starts the day you add it)

» Every morning (starts at 9 a.m.)

» Every evening (starts at 7 p.m.)

» Every 3 days (or any number of days you select)

» Every 2nd Friday (or any combination of numbers or specific days)

» Every 20th (or any day of the month)

You can get very creative with the one-time or recurring due dates that you create in Todoist. Using them wisely, you can create reminders and notifications for every aspect of your life to facilitate that *mind like water* concept that David Allen discusses.

No longer will you have to worry about all that you need to complete. Instead, Todoist will act like a personal assistant who reminds you of everything—freeing up your mind to focus on the important tasks in front of you.

Text Formatting: The final feature of the task screen is you can make your text stand out by adding a few characters. Here are a few examples:

- » **Bold**: **Text goes here**
- » *Italic*: *Text goes here*
- » ***Bold & Italic***: ** *Text goes here* **
- » Link: [Hypertext](http://www.developgoodhabits.com/) or http://www.developgoodhabits.com/ (Hypertext)
- » Emojis: Simply upload an emoji from your phone or tablet into the task.

Completing and Editing Tasks

It's easy to mark a task as completed. Depending on your platform, you'll either select the checkmark or the radio button then the task will be marked as completed in your task list and any project it's associated with.

If you need to *edit* an existing task, that's not hard to do either. Simply select the pencil image on the task, and you'll see a few options to change the project, due date, level of priority, or even add a comment. You can see what this looks like in the image below:

Comments: Add (or delete) multimedia files to the task.

Edit: Update the task to change the description, project, label, or priority, or to add a reminder.

Schedule: Change the due date of the task.

More: On most devices, this is represented by three dots (…). With this menu, you can add new tasks above or below the existing task, pin it to your start menu, archive it, or delete it.

Reminders: You can create reminders to complete a specific task. These are similar to the "push notifications" you often see on cell phones—a message will pop up reminding you to complete a specific activity.

You can set up a reminder in one of two ways:

> » *on a time and date* when the reminder will pop up

> » *on a location* where you can use Todoist's map tool to trigger the reminder

The location reminder is a premium feature that can help you create complex reminders. Specifically, it can act as a trigger to complete a positive habit in certain locations. For instance, you can use this feature to create a reminder to review your list of important tasks whenever you walk into your work location, or you can trigger a different reminder to drink water when you head into your local gym.

If you're someone who frequently struggles with remembering all those habits you'd like to build, then Todoist can help you do it! And speaking of habits, let me go over a strategy you can use with tasks to build habits into your daily routine.

How to Use the Task Feature to Build Habits

I believe there is too much "digital noise" in our modern world. From social media to app push notifications, we have become a society that's far too connected to our technology. As such, I think it's important to limit the number of apps and software programs you use daily. This brings me to another reason I love Todoist—you can use this app to build and reinforce habits.

Why Todoist Is the Perfect Trigger

There are many excellent apps that can help you build habits—one of my favorites is Coach.me. That said, I no longer use it because of something called "app overwhelm."

When you need multiple apps to run your life, it's easy to feel stressed because each piece of technology represents yet another "thing" you need to do daily. Not only does this cause a feeling of overwhelm, it also limits your ability to focus on what's truly important in your life. So, while I love Coach.me, I feel that you can easily build habits by using the Todoist app.

The reason I recommend Todoist is because of its push notification feature, which acts as a "trigger" to complete a specific action. As I mentioned in my book *Habit Stacking*, a trigger is a cue that uses one of your five senses (sight, sound, smell, touch, or taste) that acts as a reminder that you need to do something.

Triggers are important because most people can't remember a large number of tasks without a reminder. So, a trigger can push you into taking action. For instance, many people use their alarm clocks or cell phones as a trigger to wake them up in the morning.

Now, there are two basic types of triggers. The first is an *external trigger* (like a cell phone alarm, a push notification, or a Post-it note on your refrigerator). External triggers work because they create a Pavlovian response (e.g., when the alarm goes off, you complete a specific task).

The second type is an *internal trigger*, which is a feeling, thought, or emotions you associate with an established habit. These are like a scratch that you must itch. For instance, if you've ever compulsively felt the need to "check in" with social media, then this action was the direct result of an internal trigger.

You can use Todoist as your central hub for all your habit-building efforts because the notifications will act as triggers. Here are a few reasons this is important:

> » You can use the reminders feature to create an external trigger that goes off at a specific time or location.

> » You can create recurring tasks that pop up daily, weekly, monthly, or any variable time that you select.

> » You have a visual reminder of the tasks (i.e., habits) that pop up daily. If you're someone who likes to complete all "open loops," then these constant visual reminders will help you check off all those important habits.

If you use Todoist every day, then you'll discover that it's not hard to build habits because you'll constantly receive reminders that reinforce these positive behaviors.

How to Build Habits with Todoist

It's not hard to set up a habit framework within Todoist. My suggestion is to create a "parent project" for all your habits and then create a separate project for three habit types: daily, weekly, and monthly. Here's how this looks in my Todoist account:

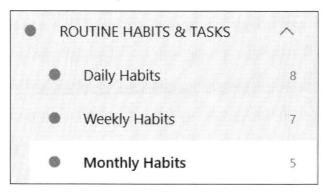

From there, you can use the recurring due date feature so the habit is scheduled at a specific day, time, or combination of both. For instance, you could create habits that automatically pop up:

» Every day at 7:00 a.m.

» Every Monday

» Every 1st of the month

» Every 14 days

You get the picture. If you review the previous section on adding tasks, then you'll see a variety of options for creating tasks that can be scheduled at a specific time or day.

Focus on Building Simple Habits

As someone who constantly thinks (and writes) about habit development, I've learned that one of the secrets to consistency is to set *realistic* daily goals. That's why I recommend creating habits that are achievable—no matter how hectic your life might get. The simplest way to do this is to incorporate a mini habits concept.

Mini habits is a term coined by my friend Stephen Guise in the book of the same name. The purpose of mini habits is to remove the resistance that you feel when it comes to starting a difficult (or time-consuming) task. It's easy to schedule an activity into your day (like running for an hour), but it's hard to complete when you feel a lack of interest.

Mini habits work because they eliminate motivation from the equation. Instead of setting an extremely challenging goal, you set a lowball goal that makes it super simple to get started. This removes any excuse for skipping a day. Examples include: *reading for one minute, exercising for five minutes,* or *eating one serving of vegetables.*

That said, what's considered a "stupidly simple" habit varies from person to person. If you're someone who struggles with habit development, then I recommend creating habits that don't require much willpower to complete daily.

On the other hand, if you're someone who only needs Todoist to reinforce an existing habit, then it's okay to create a challenging but doable goal. For instance, I focus on five core habits that I strive to do daily:

1. Write for at least 30 minutes.
2. Get 5,000 steps of movement.

3. Read nonfiction books for at least 20 minutes.

4. Complete a morning habit stacking routine.

5. Complete a post-workout habit stack.

For the first three habits, I aim to do much, *much* more than these lowball goals. But I have found that there are certain days when I don't have a lot of time (like on vacation), so having these simple goals makes them easy to complete—even if my life is crazy busy.

When it comes to creating habits in Todoist, my advice is to pick a target metric that's super easy for *you* to do every day. The target number doesn't matter. What's important is that you can do it unless there's a major personal emergency.

How to Use Todoist to Build Habit Stacks

I've mentioned habit stacking a few times already, so let me briefly explain this concept.

A habit stacking routine can be broken down into five critical components:

1. *Identify small important actions that you need to do daily.*

2. *Group these actions together into a routine.*

3. *Schedule a specific time each day to complete this routine.*

4. *Use a trigger as a reminder to complete this stack.*

5. *Make it super easy to get started.*

Since you already know that you can use the Todoist reminders feature to create triggers, let me point out another feature that can build on your habit development efforts—*Comments.*

A habit stack isn't made up on the spot. It should be a set of actions that *you* determine ahead of time that are personally important. This means putting each habit into a step-by-step checklist that you'll refer to constantly. And the best place to put this checklist is in the Comments section of a task.

As an example, here's the checklist I include in Todoist for my morning stack:

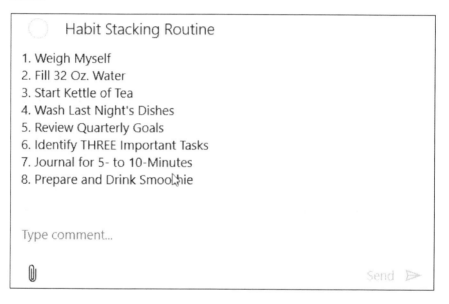

If you'd like to use Todoist to create a habit stack, then my suggestion is to put each action into one of the recurring tasks. That way, when the recurring habit is scheduled in Todoist, you can simply view the checklist of actions within the task—instead of keeping it in a separate location or on a piece of paper or in a separate app (like Evernote).

Well, that's how to use Todoist to build habits. Now let's talk about other types of tasks you can create in this app.

5 Types of Todoist Tasks

Okay, this where it might get a little confusing, so stick with me here.

At its core, Todoist is a task management app. It's best used to write down every action that needs to be completed or any idea that pops into your head. The general term I've used so far for any item entered into the app is *task*. But from my experience, there are many different types of tasks that go into Todoist.

In this section, I'll briefly cover five types of tasks:

» Actions

» Appointments

» Ideas

» Projects

» Processes

And I will explain why it's important to create a distinction between each one.

Actions: These are the quick tasks that don't require a lot of advanced planning. They can be completed in a single block of time—anywhere from a minute to a few hours. Most of the time, actions are those random activities that pop up during the week that need to be scheduled into your calendar.

Examples include:

» writing a quick report

» getting a haircut

» mowing the lawn

» going to the post office to mail a package

» handling an unexpected customer service issue

Actions can also include *habits*. As we've discussed, these are the recurring personal and professional activities you need to do daily.

Examples include:

» checking and responding to email

» writing for business or for fun

» reading nonfiction books

» exercising for at least 30 minutes

» completing an evening "shutdown" routine

Appointments: This one is pretty obvious—some tasks require you to be at a certain place at a certain time and meet with a specific person (or group of people). Generally speaking, there's no wiggle room when it comes to completing an appointment-based task. It needs to be scheduled into your calendar, and then everything else in your life has to be worked around it.

Examples include:

» doctor and dental appointments

» conversations with your lawyer, accountant, agent, or other professionals

» business meetings

» events for family members

» planned vacations

You can use Todoist to schedule these appointments at a specific day and time, but unfortunately the app doesn't have a calendar feature that lets you look at your schedule from a weekly or monthly perspective.

The good news is that Todoist *does* sync with tools like Google Calendar. This means that anything that goes on your Google Calendar will automatically show up as a Todoist task. I'll show you how to set this up in a later section.

Ideas: We all have great ideas. They often come out of nowhere—popping into your mind at the weirdest moments, like when you're exercising, showering, doing chores, and talking to others. It doesn't matter *when* or *where* you get an idea—what's important is to capture it! And one place you can capture these ideas is in Todoist.

Examples include:

- » tasks you need to complete
- » future projects to pursue
- » strategies to add to your current projects
- » people you should network with or meet
- » resources to research

The possibilities are endless when you use Todoist as an idea capture device.

Now, let me be honest here—I typically use the Evernote app to store all my ideas. I find that Evernote is a better platform for capturing certain items (like receipts, website bookmarks, audio notes, and other types of research). But since my Todoist app is always open, I'll often use it as temporary storage. When an idea pops into my head, I'll immediately put it in Todoist. Then at the end of the day, I'll either add it to an existing project or record it in Evernote as a potential project to pursue.

Whether you use Todoist, Evernote, a journal, or even a scrap of paper, it's important that you develop the habit of recording every idea that you have. You never know when a random thought will turn into a million-dollar idea!

Projects: Many tasks will require multiple actions to complete. Sometimes these can be done in a single day, and other times you'll need to spend weeks, *even months*, doing them. That's why you should turn every multi-step activity into an action-oriented project list.

This project list can include items like:

- » a due date, if there's a deadline involved—including milestones for phases of the project
- » simple tasks that can be completed in a single day,
- » clearly identifiable "next steps" that might prevent the project from moving forward
- » labels that add context about *where* the task needs to be completed, *how long* it will take, or *who* needs to be involved
- » links and resources that you want to research
- » daily habits critical to the success of the project

As you'll see later, projects are a major feature of Todoist, so we'll cover this topic in a lot more detail. But for now, here are a few examples of tasks that can be turned into a project:

- » buying a gift for a specific person

» preparing for a speech

» tackling a new work project

» training for an athletic event (like your first 5K race or an obstacle course race)

» planning a trip for your family

Processes: It's important to create a distinction between *projects* and *processes*. With a project, you often don't know what steps are needed to complete it. You start with a rough idea and keep adding tasks to the project as you think of them.

On the other hand, with a process, you've previously completed these actions before, so all you're doing is following a familiar blueprint. The goal of a process is to create a checklist so you don't miss an important step along the way.

As an example, when I first started writing books, I didn't know what I didn't know. Instead, I did a lot of research and made educated guesses about what needed to be done. As a result, my early project lists were a mix of random ideas, specific actions, and half-formed thoughts.

Now that I've published dozens of books, I've boiled everything down to a step-by-step process. All I have to do is load up my list to Todoist, complete each task, and once this checklist is complete … voila! I have a completed book.

So how can *you* make a distinction between projects and processes?

Well, once you've completed a similar project once or twice, then you won't need to create a brand-new project list because all the actions will be familiar. Instead, all you'll need is a checklist (i.e., a process) to remind you of all the steps to complete.

And the best part?

You can create a process list one time, upload it to Todoist, and then you'll have a paint-by-numbers checklist that you're familiar with. Once again, this is a topic we'll cover extensively in a future section. Until then, here are a few examples of processes:

» going grocery shopping

» packing for a trip

» preparing for your weekly meeting

» writing a book

» publishing a blog post

Well, there you have it: five types of tasks that can be included in Todoist. Now let's move on and talk about why it's crucial to identify your most important tasks and work on these actions before anything else.

How to Focus on Your Most Important Tasks (MITs)

It's easy to feel overwhelmed if your day starts with dozens of tasks and appointments. You can simplify everything by identifying the tasks that have the biggest impact on your career or life, then do them first thing in the morning. These are often called the *Most Important Tasks* or MITs for short.

My suggestion is to pick one to three MITs that absolutely must be completed by the end of the day. Two should relate to an urgent project with an immediate deadline, and one should be part of a long-term goal.

For instance, many years ago, I determined that one of my core 80/20 activities is writing. So, even if I have a bunch of urgent tasks that are due at the end of the day, I always set aside at least 30 minutes for this task—usually right after my morning routine. From there, I spend the rest of my morning on the other two MITs.

By focusing on important activities right away, I create an energized state that allows me to work on any project in the afternoon.

Todoist makes it super simple to identify your MITs. Get started by reviewing your list of upcoming tasks in the morning. Then identify the three that will have the biggest impact on your life and rank them, using the Priority feature in Todoist:

  » MIT #1 (red flag priority)
  » MIT #2 (orange flag priority)

» MIT #3 (yellow flag priority)

These MITs will be displayed at the top of your task list, (right below any time-specific appointments.) This provides a great visual reminder of the specific items that need to be completed for that day.

> **Warning:** As a reminder, be careful with the priorities feature. A task should only be labeled as a priority if it's time sensitive or is a task that is crucial to your long-term success. The danger is if you identify all your tasks as priorities, then you'll be confused about what task needs to be worked on first.

Don't underestimate the value of the simple concept of MITs. Whereas most people start their day engaged in trivial activities (i.e., checking email, browsing social media, or attending meetings), you can hit the ground running by knocking off the tasks that have the biggest impact on your career or personal life.

Trust me: There's no greater feeling in the world then reaching the afternoon knowing that you've already checked off the biggest task from your to-do list.

Should You Focus on Todoist Zero?

Before we move on, let me talk briefly about a concept called "Todoist Zero" and how it can limit your productivity.

I'll be the first to admit that it's fun to complete dozens of tasks in a single day. There's something motivating about starting the day with a lengthy list of tasks and then systematically checking them off. You end the day feeling like you've really accomplished something.

Todoist encourages this behavior by notifying others that you've achieved *Todoist Zero*—completed all the items on your list—by sharing the #todoistzero on social media.

But in the immortal words of Admiral Ackbar, "It's a Trap!"

You see, the danger of focusing on Todoist Zero is you're emphasizing *quantity over quality*. In the Todoist world, it's better to complete 30 quick tasks than it is to complete three quality tasks. Todoist even rewards this behavior by awarding you with Karma points.

I call this "checklist porn" because it's a low-value activity that emphasizes the trivial over what truly matters. In my humble opinion, a to-do list should help you focus on the big-picture items instead of checking off dozens of random tasks.

My point?

It's not necessary to complete every task that you've scheduled for the day. Instead, if you've completed all your MITs and scheduled appointments, then it's perfectly okay to *not* achieve Todoist Zero. Just reschedule any unfinished tasks for tomorrow and pick up where you left off.

Now that you know how to create tasks in Todoist, let's move on and talk about how to sort tasks into projects. This is yet another way to make sure that your days are spent working on activities that truly add significance to your life.

PROJECTS: A Simple Feature for Organizing Your Tasks

A Brief Explanation of Projects

So far, we've only briefly discussed projects, but now let's dive into the weeds and talk about this Todoist feature.

In my opinion, any task that requires multiple steps to complete should be put into its own project. That way, you can break everything down into actionable steps that can be completed daily.

At the very least, you should create a project for every major area of your life. One idea is to create a project for the seven primary areas of your life:

1. **Career:** Goals that help you focus on improving your productivity, increasing your business revenue, or climbing up the proverbial corporate ladder. Whether you're looking to improve a specific work-related skill or streamline your business, career goals are important because they have a direct impact on the other six areas of your life.

2. **Finance:** Goals that will increase in importance as you get older. These actions include saving for retirement, improving your credit score, eliminating your credit card debt, and investing to build long-term wealth.

3. **Health:** Goals help you maintain a balance of physical fitness and eating the right foods. There are many subcategories that are included here, like losing weight, improving your diet, eating different types of foods, or becoming more physically active.

4. **Leisure:** Goals that relate to personally significant activities. Often, we feel overwhelmed by everything else in life, so we

procrastinate on those "bucket list" items that don't seem immediately important. However, the best way to improve the quality of your life is to set goals that relate to the fun stuff. These activities can include planning vacations, spending time with your family, or focusing on a hobby like home brewing, hunting, cooking, or painting.

5. **Relationships:** Goals that are about enhancing relationships with your significant other, family members, or friends. You could also set goals to improve your social skills, find a romantic partner, or simply become a better person to everyone you meet.

6. **Service:** Goals that are about helping others through volunteering, supporting your favorite charity, or donating money to causes you believe in.

7. **Spirituality:** Goals in this category have a different meaning for each of us. They could include activities like meditation, prayer, yoga, or reciting affirmations. Basically, whatever helps you achieve a calm peace of mind can be categorized as a spiritual goal.

Really, how you structure your projects is up to you. What I like to do is focus on a few core projects at a time and schedule my tasks around these goals. To get an idea of how this looks, here is a snapshot of my Todoist account:

Projects	Labels	Filters

Book Projects ∧

    Book Marketing & Ideas   43

    Procrastination Book   12

    ToDoist Mastery   63

    Upgrade Your Lifestyle   75

Develop Good Habits Blog ∨

Home & Personal Projects   26

IRONMAN Training   1

Backburner Projects   1 ∨

+ Add Project

The way that I structure my Todoist account is by sorting my tasks in seven primary buckets. The first are the habits I'd like to build using Todoist as a reminder. This is represented in the parent project, *Routine Habits & Tasks*.

Next, there are four current projects I'm focusing on:

1. Book Projects

2. Develop Good Habits Blog

3. Home & Personal Projects

4. IRONMAN Training

Finally, there is a parent project called "Backburner Projects," which are projects that I'm temporarily putting on hold.

The key to structuring is to organize these projects together in what are called "parent projects."

Parent Projects (and Why You Should Use Them)

A parent project is a top-level folder that contains individual projects within it. You would typically use a parent project for any area of your life where you have to juggle multiple projects at once.

For instance, let's say you have a parent project of "Finances." Within this category, you could create individual projects like: *Debt reduction*, *Investments*, *Future Home Purchase*, and *Taxes*. Technically, all can be organized under the umbrella of finances, but putting them into a different project helps you laser-focus on the specific goal you'd like to achieve for each one.

To further illustrate this concept, refer to the previous image of my projects. I've broken down the career area of my life into two parent projects—*Book Projects* and *Develop Good Habits Blog*.

In the *Book Projects* parent project, I've created a separate project for each of my current books and another one for book marketing strategies I'd like to implement:

- » Book Marketing & Ideas
- » Procrastination Book (also known as *"The Anti-Procrastination Habit"*)
- » Master Todoist (the book you're currently reading)
- » Upgrade Your Lifestyle (the book I'm writing next)

In the Develop Good Habits Blog folder, I've broken down this massive goal into three separate projects:

- » Growth Hacking Ideas
- » Content Creation & SEO (search engine optimization)
- » Email Funnels

I won't waste your time providing a detailed explanation of the tasks inside each of these projects. Suffice to say, the best way to organize your Todoist projects is to create a few parent projects for your life and then smaller projects for each major goal you'd like to accomplish.

How to Create New Projects

It's super simple to add your own projects. Just scroll down to the bottom of the project list and look for the option that says: *+ Add Project.* Tap or click this button to see this option:

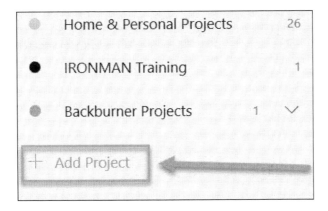

» **New project name:** Pick a name that's related to a specific goal you'd like to accomplish (this will help you remember why this project is personally important to you).

» **Color:** Choose from 28 different options for this project.

» **Shared:** Add team members that will collaborate on this project.

» **Parent:** Pick a parent project where this new project will go or pick "no parent" to make it a top-level project.

Like most features in Todoist, these menu options are self-explanatory, but the next set of instructions can be a little confusing, so pay close attention to the next section.

How to Edit Projects

If you tap or click on any project, you'll have the option to edit it. Unfortunately, this feature can be confusing because each platform has different options (and terminology) for editing projects.

For instance, the two platforms that I use to access Todoist are the Windows 10 app and iPhone. When I edit projects in Windows 10, I see these options:

But when I fire up my iPhone, I see these options:

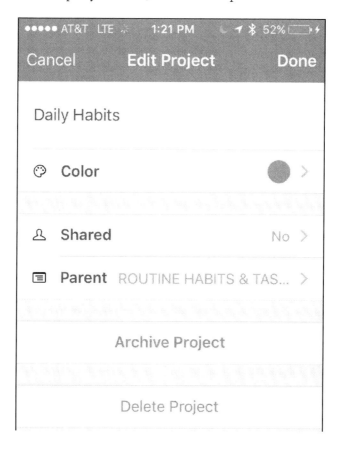

Don't worry if what you see in this section is different than what's displayed on *your* screen. As always, if you play around with the Todoist app for a few minutes, it's not hard to figure out the buttons.

Regardless of what platform you use, you should see these options in the *Edit Project* screen.

» **Add Task:** Create tasks that will be added automatically to the bottom of the project.

» **Project Comments:** Create a description of the project and why it's important, and upload multimedia files (i.e., images, audio, computer files, and even emojis) from your device.

» **Share:** Give permission to a team member to access this project so he or she can be assigned tasks. You can do this by typing the name or email address of the recipient.

» **Sort:** Organize the tasks in a project using three options: *Sort by date, sort by priority,* or *sort by name.*

» **Edit Project:** Change the name of the project, the project color, and who it's shared with.

» **Pin to Start:** Add this project to the start menu of your computer, which helps you instantly access the project. (This is a limited option only available on a few platforms—like Windows 10.)

» **Delete:** Remove the project and all the tasks included in it.

» **Archive Project:** Remove the project from your list of current projects, but it's still kept in Todoist—just in case you want to access the project at a later point.

» **Export to Template:** Take your current lists of tasks and turn it into a CSV file that can be used as a project in the future. This is a killer premium feature that I'll discuss in the next section.

» **Import to Template:** Take an existing file on your computer and add it to an existing project. This is the perfect solution for anyone who likes to use processes throughout their personal and professional life. Again, we'll cover this feature soon.

» **Completed Tasks:** Look at the lists of all the actions you've "checked off" for that project and the date of when it was completed.

» **Search Tasks:** Enter a keyword or phrase to find a specific task.

» **Activity Log:** Look at the tasks you've completed and any new items that have recently been added to this list.

That's a brief overview of how to add projects and edit them. Now let's move on and talk about five advanced strategies you can use to maximize your productivity when it comes to managing projects.

5 Strategies for Creating Actionable Projects

As you can see, you can do many things with the projects feature. But to get the most from Todoist, you should create a framework where you focus on what's important and ignore everything else. Here are five strategies that can help you do this.

Strategy #1: Focus on Five Projects

The common mistake that people make with their to-do lists is they create projects for every goal they'd like to achieve *someday*. This can cause a feeling of overwhelm because you'll end up with dozens of projects without a clear action plan for what to work on first.

That's why I recommend a simple strategy: instead of managing dozens of projects in Todoist, I suggest limiting your focus to just a few core areas of your life.

As an example, my *current* five focuses (in order of priority) are:

1. Being present with friends and family
2. Completing an IRONMAN race
3. Writing and marketing my books
4. Increasing web traffic to my blog, DevelopGoodHabits.com, and converting visitors into email subscribers
5. Fixing and updating sections of my home

It's not written in stone that you concentrate only on five projects. You could have a few more or a few less. The important thing is to proactively think about your time, commitments and where you spend the most time. If every one of your actions is directly aligned with a goal, then you'll feel excited to do it, which helps you create to-do lists that get results.

The benefit of switching to a "five core projects" focus is it's easy to make decisions about the tasks you *choose* to complete. You start each day with a 5- to 10-minute review and pick the activities that will help you make progress on your important goals.

(Focusing on five projects is a concept that I talk about extensively in my book, *The Anti-Procrastination Habit*. So if you'd like to know how this strategy can help improve your productivity and overall happiness in life, then I encourage you to check out this book.)

Strategy #2: Create a "Backburner" Parent Project List

I know focusing on five projects might be a bit extreme. Like many people, you're probably someone who has an extensive list of goals and aspirations that don't fit neatly into a handful of goals. So if you feel there is a goal that you'd like to pursue *soon*, but not right now, then I recommend creating a project for it and then organizing it under a parent project list titled, "Backburner."

The logic behind this strategy is you'll have a place to put any tasks/ ideas related to this project, but you also won't feel the impulse to work on them while you're focusing on your current five projects.

Think back to the *mind like water* concept that I mentioned at the beginning of the book. You want to get every idea out of your head, so you can focus on what's in front of you. With the backburner strategy, you capture an idea, put it in a folder for that goal, and then be confident that this task will be there when you're ready to work on that particular goal.

To illustrate this point, here are four projects that are in my backburner parent project list:

» finances/investing

» real estate investing

» physical product

» networking project

The first two (finances/investing and real estate investing) are projects that I've previously worked on. Right now, there's nothing I can do to make progress on either goal. For example, for my *real estate investing* project, I haven't found a new house that I'd like to purchase, so there's no action that's required to work on this project. But as soon as I find something worth buying, then I'll make this project "active" and commit to working on it daily.

The last two projects (physical product and networking) are related to goals that I'd *like* to work on soon, but I don't have the time to do so in the next few months. That said, I'll occasionally have ideas that might be important, so they go into these projects and will be there when I have the time to follow up on them.

Managing your life through a backburner project list is a simple way to make sure that you don't miss anything while preventing that feeling of overwhelm whenever you try to manage dozens of daily obligations.

Strategy #3: Create a "Someday/Maybe" Project

Another project list you can have in Todoist is a "Someday/Maybe" list. This is another *Getting Things Done* concept that helps you capture all the open loops in your life.

If you're like many people, you frequently have great ideas but not the time to work on them. You know you'd like to do them someday—just not in the immediate future. With a Someday/Maybe list, you can capture these ideas without feeling pressured to work on them immediately.

The Someday/Maybe project is kind of like a bucket list—it's a central place where you put all the actions you might be interested in doing down the road. These are things like:

- » the vacation you want to go on with your family
- » that book you've always wanted to write
- » the work project that you'd focus on
- » the part of your home that you'd like to remodel
- » the challenging race you'd like to train for

Unlike the other projects in Todoist, most entries in the Someday/Maybe list aren't actionable. If you're focusing on your five core projects, then you probably won't have time to do anything with these ideas. But having them in one place can be great for those times when you complete one project and need something new to work on.

Be sure to continuously add to the Someday/Maybe list. This is a place where you think big about what you want from life. And whenever you complete one project, you can review this list and pick a new one.

Strategy #4: Turn Projects into Processes

As I've discussed, if you have a recurring project with a similar list of steps, then you should consider turning it into a process. You can do this by creating a template and uploading it to Todoist whenever you have to start a new project.

As an example, it takes over 80 individual actions (in addition to daily writing) to publish one of these books. It would take a *long time* to manually enter these tasks into Todoist. But since I keep all the steps in a single file, all I have to do is create a project for each book, upload the process file to the book-specific project, and then I automatically have a sequential list of the actions that need to be completed.

It's not hard to turn a project into a process. In fact, you can do it in five steps that only take a few minutes to complete.

#1. Identify any project that has a repeatable list of actions. You can do this for any area of your personal or professional life. The only requirement is it should be something that you'll do at least once or twice a year. For instance, you could create a process to:

» Plan an upcoming trip—including items like booking a flight/ hotel, reserving a car, and researching the area you're traveling to.

» Pack for a trip where you create a checklist of all the items that you need to bring with you. Do this for both business trips *and* your vacations.

» Prepare for a business meeting or conference.

» Complete a work-related project that occurs every week or month.

» Set up a checklist that you follow for any set of actions related to your job.

» Create a grocery list of all the items you typically purchase. You can upload the same template, do a quick review of what you have on hand, and then purchase the remainder at the store.

» Follow a recipe of your favorite meal.

The choices are infinite here. You can easily turn dozens of processes that you regularly complete into a project template. Just think of the different areas of your life and turn each recurring activity into a process.

Never underestimate the power of checklists. Not only do they help people stay organized, but they also save lives. For more on this, I highly recommend *The Checklist Manifesto* by Atul Gawande, which talks about how simple checklists have been proven to save lives in the airline and medical industries.

#2. Create the process in a simple file. The simplest way to do this is to open a spreadsheet program (like Microsoft Excel), put each step in a separate row, and then save this list as a .CSV file.

The key here is to turn these tasks into a step-by-step sequence. This is important because Todoist will create tasks based on the order they show up in the file. So think of all the tasks that are required and make sure they follow a logical flow.

#3. Upload the project to Todoist. This feature isn't available on some devices (like the iPhone), so I recommend uploading this template from a Mac or Windows computer. Simply find the CSV file on your computer and upload it.

Here's an example of how this would look:

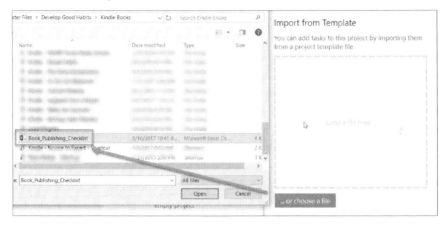

#4. Review the list that you've just imported. Make sure the items are in sequential order and that each task has an easy-to-identify next step. If a task is out of order, you can drag and drop it and put it in the correct sequence in this list.

#5. If you already have a project in Todoist that you want to turn into a process, you can export it into a template. This is a useful technique if you feel that a current project might be important sometime in the future. You can simply take this project and turn into a downloadable file.

There are two ways to export a file:

1. Export to a file where you can download the steps in a .CSV file.

2. Export to a URL where you can share the project template with team members.

Using templates for any repeatable process removes a lot of the guesswork that happens with productivity. Instead of wondering about what actions you need to complete, you can open up your process list and follow it like a checklist.

Strategy #5: Ask Yourself: "What's the Next Action?"

Another concept from *Getting Things Done* that works well with Todoist is to frequently ask yourself "What's the next action?" whenever looking at a project. There are a few reasons why this is a valuable question to ask:

» It forces you to take action on projects that often sit in Todoist without you doing anything about it. Asking this question forces you to think about the single task you can do *right now* to move a project forward.

» It makes you clarify each step because you'll often create steps that don't have an actual clearly identifiable step. Most of the time people will have a vague description without any sort of action plan behind it.

For instance, you might have "plan vacation" as a step in your project. But when you force yourself to ask the "What's my next action?" question, you can clarify this task and turn it into a starting task like, "Brainstorm 10 vacation destinations."

» It forces you to *actually* take action. We've all had those projects that we dread because they seem challenging or insurmountable. The result is you keep putting them off. But when you identify a simple task that you can do to move a project forward, it forces you into action.

Even if you don't have the entire project mapped out, you'll at least know what you need to do to move it forward. All you need to do is ask yourself "What's my next action?"

My recommendation is to review all your current projects at least once a week. Go through all the tasks you've created, asking yourself "What's my next action?" Or more importantly, "What is the simplest thing I can do right now to create momentum?"

If you commit yourself to asking these probing questions, you'll discover that even the most challenging project can be broken down into a series of *doable* steps.

Finally, after reviewing this list and identifying those next steps, you can use the *Label* feature of Todoist to mark them as @Next. This helps you create a simple index of all the tasks that are the bottlenecks preventing you from making forward progress on a project.

Up to this point, we haven't talked much about the Labels feature (and another feature called Filters), so I'll go over them in the next section and show you how these advanced features can help you focus on what's important.

LABELS AND FILTERS: How to Create Dynamic Lists in Todoist

Why Labels Are Important

Earlier in the book, I mentioned two other tabs that are displayed next to the Projects feature—*Labels* and *Filters*.

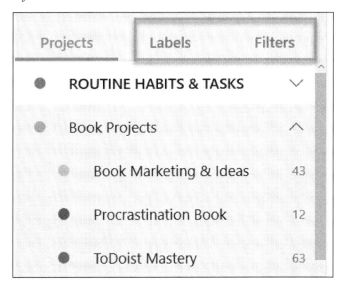

On the surface, both might seem unimportant for your task management efforts. But if you're someone who frequently juggles numerous projects, then these two features can be a game changer when it comes to identifying the most important tasks that you need to complete *right now*.

So let's talk about labels first, and then we'll dive into filters.

Labels are best used to batch similar tasks together—regardless of what project they are in. You can use labels to identify tasks that require the same type of action to complete them.

As an example, let's say you create a label like @phone. When you find yourself with an hour block of free time, you can pull up all the tasks related to this task and create an impromptu checklist of all the phone calls you need to make.

Labels are also great for adding context to your to-do lists. They could describe the location where you need to complete a task, or how much time is required, or the people who need to be involved, or if you're waiting for a specific action to be completed before you can take that next step with a project.

You can create a label for any type of context. Here are a number of examples:

» @next: the "what's my next action" task in a project to move it forward

» @5_min: tasks that only take a few minutes to complete

» @phone: phone calls you need to make

» @waiting: if you're waiting for a certain action to be completed before you can complete this item

» @home: actions that need to be completed at home

» @work: actions that need to be completed at work

» @www: any task that should require looking things up while on the web

» @review: actions where something just needs to be read or reviewed (perfect for waiting in lines)

» @school: actions that need to be completed at school

» @email: correspondence that needs to be sent via email

» @laptop: work done at your laptop or PC

» @mobile: done on your mobile phone (social media, etc.), which is another good batch you can use while waiting for appointments or in line

» @phone: any work that needs to be done via phone calls

» @errands: all the shopping, personal appointments, or any task that needs to be completed when you're in your car

» @meetings: any task related to a work or personal meeting

» @daily: any recurring daily task

» @weekly: any recurring weekly task

» @monthly: any recurring monthly task

Here is an example of a few labels that I use:

Projects	Labels	Filters
▶ Phone		
▶ 5_Min		
▶ Home		
▶ Errands		
▶ Meetings		
▶ Email		
▶ **Kristin**		
+ Add Label		

It's not hard to add a label. Just tap or click the + *Add Label* button that's at the bottom when you're in the label tab. Simply create a name for it (my advice is to use simple names like I just described) and then pick a color for that label.

Once you've created a label, you can include it in all future and existing tasks. It's really easy to do this. Simply type the @ symbol in a task, and you'll see a drop menu of all the labels you've previously created. Just pick one that is the most relevant and add it to the task.

Finally, if you want to find all the labels you've created, you have two options:

1. Go directly to the labels tab and look at the lists you've created.

2. Type the name of the label in the search bar—without the @ symbol. In other words, you should search using the term *meetings* instead of *@meetings*.

Labels are a great way to compile tasks that have similar actions but might not be in the same project. If you're someone who'd like to organize your time using the time blocking technique that we'll talk about soon, then I recommend adding a label whenever you create a task.

Why Filters Are Important

Another great feature of Todoist is a concept called Filters. Filters allow you to find tasks that match a specific criterion in seconds—like tasks that are due at a specific time.

Filters are best used in combination with labels. Both are extremely useful for the professional who has a complex collection of projects and processes. They can help you narrow down your list of tasks and identify actions that need to be completed immediately.

The main goal of filters is to create a list of similar tasks like you would do with a label, but they are a little more sophisticated because you can create lists using keywords, priorities, and time.

To create a filter, simply go to the + *Filters* button at the bottom of the filters section tab, or the bottom left corner if you're on a mobile device.

Here you're given three options for creating a filter:

1. **Filter name:** Create a name that makes it easy to understand the context of the filter.

2. **Filter query:** Add a term or combination of terms that will tell Todoist to search through your tasks, projects, and labels to come up with a specific batch of tasks.

3. **Filter color:** Pick a specific color that will represent that filter.

The first and third options are self-explanatory, but let's talk about queries because this feature can be confusing to many first-time Todoist users—myself included.

Time Filter Queries

Time filters is the most common command that most people will use. You can input any date, time, or combination of both to create a filter that will show tasks with a specific deadline. The date formulas you use are the same ones you'd use when creating a task.

For example:

- » August 26
- » Tomorrow
- » Today
- » In 20 days
- » Monday
- » 26 Aug 2017

You can also pull off tasks that are due before or after a specific date. All the following options can be used to run a query:

- » due before: August 26
- » due before: 26/8
- » due before: 7pm today
- » due after: August 26
- » due after: 26/8

The list of query commands is rounded out by the final single use time parameters:

- » No date: Shows all task with no date assigned
- » Overdue: Shows all tasks overdue
- » 10 days: Shows all tasks due within ten days
- » Recurring: All tasks that have a recurring due date

Assignment Filter Queries

The next type of filter that can be created is an assignment filter. These are best used when working with team members. The goal of this filter is to find the tasks that have been handed off to others through Todoist, tasks you've assigned to yourself, and tasks that haven't been assigned.

The assignment "names" can be any name you give to the system. Just be consistent with these naming conventions. For instance, if you assign a task to "Joseph," then Todoist won't be able to find tasks that "Joe" is working on.

In place of a name, you can also use email addresses to assign and find tasks. Yet again, the important thing is to be consistent with how you refer to others when assigning tasks and running a filter query.

Here are a few examples of assignment filters you can create:

» **Assigned to:** Others—Shows all tasks that have been assigned to anyone but yourself

» **Assigned by:** Joe—Shows all tasks that have been assigned by "Joe"

» **Assigned to:** VA—Shows all tasks assigned to another person, like your virtual assistant (or VA)

» **Assigned**—Shows all tasks that have been assigned to anyone at all

» **Shared**—Shows all tasks in "shared projects"

Priority Level Filter Queries

As I've discussed, Todoist comes with four types of priorities—the default "no priority" filter and the three levels of priorities. With a filter, you can run a query to see only the tasks that are either a priority 1, priority 2, or priority 3, or no priority—across all your projects.

This query is useful if you'd like to complete your most important tasks. You can run a filter that identifies your top priorities and use this as a list of tasks that need to be worked on before anything else.

Keyword Filter Queries

These work similarly to labels. You can create a group of tasks that contain a specific phrase either in the task or in the comments section, then the filter will only display these tasks.

For example, if I created a filter titled *Email*, then I can pull up all the tasks that have the word email in it and then work on completing just these tasks. This is useful for those times when you block off time to do just one type of activity.

It's easy to create a keyword filter query. Simply type the phrase *search: KEYWORD (and substitute* KEYWORD with the phrase that would help you find these specific types of tasks). Then you'll have a list of tasks that require a similar type of action to complete.

Putting It All Together: Projects, Labels, and Filters

By now, you should have a good handle on how projects, filters, and labels work in Todoist. What's missing is how to use them together so that you're focusing on the tasks that truly matter. That's why in this section I'll go over a few strategies you can use to create unique filters that help you focus on your most important tasks.

If you get stuck with any of these commands, I recommend checking out the support article on the Todoist site: https://support.todoist.com/hc/en-us/articles/205248842-Filters

How to Create Priority Filters

Like I said before, out of the box, Todoist has four ways to prioritize tasks—three priority levels and a "no priority" option. By default, you can use a filter query that lists all the tasks underneath that priority. The tasks that are imminent and overdue will also show up near the top of this priority list.

That's pretty helpful, but we can do a little bit better if you use a simple decision-making strategy called the Eisenhower Matrix. (Stephen Covey, author of *The 7 Habits of Highly Effective People,* further popularized Eisenhower's concept by supporting Eisenhower's use of four quadrants to determine the urgency of one's tasks.)

The Eisenhower Matrix prioritizes your tasks by urgency and importance, which results in four quadrants that each require a separate approach and strategy. In addition to sorting tasks by urgency and importance, the matrix also identifies tasks that you should either delegate or completely remove from your life. Following is a brief overview of how this looks.

Quadrant 1 (Q1): Urgent and Important are the "do first" tasks because they are critical for your life or career in some way and need to be finished right away. They are the tasks that need to be done in order to avoid negative consequences. It's important to be able to manage the tasks that are in Q1 before anything else, so you want to get these tasks done as soon as possible.

Quadrant 2 (Q2): Important but Not Urgent are the "decide when" tasks because, while they can have an amazing impact on your life, they don't seem immediately critical like the Q1 tasks that need to be done right away.

Quadrant 3 (Q3): Urgent but Not Important are the "delegate it" tasks because, while they seem urgent, they can often be automated or passed off to someone who is better qualified to handle them.

Quadrant 4 (Q4): Not Important and Not Urgent are the "delete it" tasks because they are the activities you should avoid at all costs. They are simply a complete waste of your time. If you are able to identify and eliminate all of your Q4 tasks, then you can free up much-needed time that can be reinvested in Q2 tasks.

Here are examples of how you create these four quadrants and the queries you'd need to type into the filter to make them work.

Quadrant 1—Urgent and Important: **(overdue, today) & (p1, p2, or p3)**

Quadrant 2—Important but Not Urgent: **(no date) & (p1, p2, or p3)**

Quadrant 3—Urgent but Not Important: **(overdue, today)**

Quadrant 4—Not Important and Not Urgent: **(no date)**

Perhaps these four quadrants are even enough for you, but you can take it one step further by layering on an additional search for your filters. Let's say you want to search for a specific task and see how you're doing with that specific task. All you need to do is add a keyword onto the end of one of the search terms.

For example, let's say I wanted to do a search of all tasks related to books and find out which tasks are important and urgent and **only related to books**.

All I need to do is make a new filter—probably titled something like "Overdue Book Tasks." Then I just use the query for important *and* urgent: Overdue, today and (p1, p2 *and* add on a modifier for the book keyword: search:books).

How to Use Filters to Batch Your Tasks

One of the best ways to structure your workweek is to batch similar tasks together, rather than jumping from project to project. For instance, you could answer all your emails once a day or set aside all your phone calls to be made in a single block of time. You could even have "theme days" where you *only* complete one type of action.

The challenge of this strategy is you need a simple way to find similar tasks across *all* your projects. This can be tricky if you don't want to add five to six labels within each task. So an alternative strategy is you can set up a filter to search for keywords used within the task.

As an example, if you wanted to find all tasks related to Twitter, you have two choices:

1. Label every task dealing with Twitter with the **@twitter** label.

2. Use the word "twitter" when writing each task relating to Twitter and make a filter that will allow you to call up all tasks relating to Twitter with one click. You could name this filter something clever like "Twitter Tasks," but the actual query use is simple: **search:twitter**.

The first choice is easier, but if you find yourself with too many labels, then the second option can help you simplify the process.

Now, if you'd like to batch similar tasks together across a variety of projects, you can use the Filter option to find similar tasks. Consider these few examples:

1. Let's say I'm supposed to start a podcast interview in seven minutes and feel like doing something productive that will help my next book project. I could run a filter query like—**search:-book & @5minutes**. This will search every task for the keyword "book" and display every task that has a label of taking less than five minutes to complete.

2. You're waiting in line at the bank, and you'd like to complete a quick task. You could simply create a filter titled "Quick" which runs a query for these labels **@mobile** or **@review**. This will find any task that can be done on your mobile phone (like updating Buffer, Twitter, etc.) or identify documents that only need to be

read and reviewed, which can be done online if docs are stored someplace like Google Drive, Dropbox, or Pocket.

3. Maybe you're tired one day and don't feel like working on important tasks. For those days, you could have a simple filter query like: Overdue & (no priority or priority 3). This shows low-priority tasks that are also overdue.

How to Use Filters to Create Tasks Based on Your Energy

Completing tasks based on your energy levels is an important part of successfully managing your time. Unfortunately, there isn't a default setting for energy levels in Todoist. That said, Mike Vardy has a great post where he talks about setting your day around energy levels. If that sounds like something you'd want to do, then you can use the Labels and Filters features to create lists based off how you feel throughout the day.

In a nutshell, Vardy recommends you put tasks into three buckets:

1. High energy
2. Normal energy
3. Low energy

High-energy tasks are the important tasks that get real results. These are the critical activities that require a lot of concentration. As such, these tasks need to be completed when you feel the most refreshed and energized.

Normal-energy tasks may not require you to be fully energized, but they shouldn't be worked on when you're feeling uninspired. Typically, these are the activities that you complete during a normal workday.

Low-energy tasks are those tasks you do while feeling tired or lethargic, or even when you have a TV on in the background. They don't take a lot of effort or brainpower.

So how do you set up a framework based on energy levels?

First, you should add a label to all your tasks like: @high, @low, or @ normal.

Next, you should make sure that your high-energy tasks are completed before moving on to the low-energy tasks. You can do this by creating filters using a mix of labels and running a filter based on a specific time parameter—like the next five days.

Here's how this would look:

» High-energy tasks: @high & 5 days

» Normal-energy tasks: @normal & 5 days

» Low-energy tasks: @low & 5 days

You can do amazing things when you combine filters and labels. If you're someone who manages multiples projects with lots of tasks that need to be completed, you can't just rely on your project lists to identify tasks. But if you combine labels and filters, you'll discover that it's not hard to create dynamic lists that combine tasks from *all* your current projects.

Congratulations!

You now understand all the core features in Todoist. At this point, you can create sophisticated to-do lists that can help you: focus on a few core projects, identify specific groups of activities, and work on what's truly important to you.

But there's one last core strategy I'd like to cover—how to schedule your workweek so you're spending time working on the tasks that will make a difference in your life.

How to Create a Weekly Schedule with Todoist

I've mentioned this already, but I need to drive home this point—completing tasks just for the sake of checking them off is *not* the secret to being productive. Sure, it's nice to get that small dopamine rush when crossing an item off your list, but the true benefit of Todoist happens when you're able to laser-focus on the actions that will have the biggest long-term impact on your life.

All of this starts when you're able to combine your tasks with a weekly schedule. A weekly schedule gives you an opportunity to identify the crucial tasks that you choose to focus on for the next seven days. And it also acts as your first line of defense against those random tasks that could potentially derail your week, causing you to feel overwhelmed.

Now, the weekly schedule isn't about cramming as many activities as possible into your calendar. Instead, it's best used to make sure you're maximizing the time spent on your Todoist tasks. That's why I recommend setting up a simple weekly schedule, using this three-step process:

Step #1: Sync Todoist with Google Calendar

Calendars are a critical part of any productive time management system. When your schedule is planned out in advance, you're less likely to respond to disruptions or succumb to those temptations to work on activities that don't directly relate to your long-term goals.

There is no perfect type of calendar to use. Some folks prefer the digital option, while others like physical calendars or weekly planners that allow them to quickly look at their entire week. That said, if you're fully committed to using Todoist to manage your tasks, then I recommend scheduling your time using an online calendar system—specifically Google Calendar.

There are three reasons why I recommend this tool:

First, it provides a quick bird's-eye view of your schedule. When completing your weekly and daily reviews (that I cover in the next two steps), you can use Google Calendar to view all your upcoming meetings, appointments, and personal obligations. This makes it easy to gauge how much time you can schedule for the priority tasks on your project list.

Next, Google Calendar syncs with the top appointment scheduling tools like Microsoft Outlook, Calendly, Acuity, and Schedule Once. So when you accept an invite for a meeting from one of these services, it can automatically block off time on your calendar. This will help you make sure that you don't double-book your time.

Third and most importantly, Google Calendar easily syncs with Todoist. Specifically, whenever a task is scheduled into Google Calendar, it will be scheduled automatically as a task in Todoist.

This is powerful stuff! What this means is you don't have to rely on dozens of apps to manage your time. All you really need is Google Calendar to plan your week and Todoist to manage those day-to-day tasks. You can start each morning by reviewing Todoist and you'll be 100% confident that all your tasks and appointments will be right in front of you.

How to Sync Google Calendar with Todoist

It's not hard to get the two tools to work with one another. In fact, there are two options (both are easy to set up).

First, you can use the If This Then That website (also known as IFTTT. com). The purpose of IFTTT is to create automated rules between two pieces of technology that you use frequently. (IFTTT calls them recipes.) One recipe that I recommend is to automatically turn your Google Calendar events into Todoist tasks. That means whenever you schedule an appointment on your calendar, it will pop up as a task in your Inbox—and it will create a reminder for that event.

This first option is perfect if want to set up the automated process within a few minutes. All you need to do is click the above link or visit IFTTT.com, verify your account with both tools, and the automation will happen instantly with all your future tasks.

The second option requires a bit more effort, but it's worth it if you want to be 100% certain that your Todoist tasks reflect your *actual* schedule.

Let me explain why this is important.

The downside of using automated recipes from IFTTT.com is it doesn't adjust when your schedule changes. If you have to switch the time of a meeting, or even cancel it, then a task will show up in Todoist that has the original information—not the new time.

Yes, this is a minor hassle for most people. But if you're a busy salesperson who lives and dies by your schedule, then this "mild inconvenience" can wreak havoc on your schedule. It could even cause you to miss an important meeting because you had incorrect information.

So if you'd like to pick the second option, then I recommend following this quick five-step process:

1. Sign in to Todoist through your preferred **web browser** (i.e., Safari, Chrome, or Firefox).

2. Click on the gear icon that's at the top right part of the page.

3. Go to the *Settings* option.

4. Click the *Integrations* tab.

5. Click the *Connect* button for Google Calendar.

After you complete this process, any task that goes into Google Calendar will automatically show up as a scheduled Todoist task. If any step of the process is confusing, then check out the quick walk-through video that's part of the free companion website.

Step #2: Use a Weekly Review to Schedule Your Tasks

The best way to identify your priority Todoist tasks is by completing a "weekly review" session. Here you will identify the crucial tasks that you choose to focus on for the next seven days, which acts as your first line of defense against those random tasks that could potentially derail your week, causing you to feel overwhelmed.

The weekly review isn't about cramming as many activities as possible into your schedule. Instead, it's best used to make sure you're maximizing the time spent on those most important projects that you've previously identified.

You can do this by completing four actions that take 30 to 60 minutes to complete:

Action #1: Answer Five Questions

Each weekly review should start with a few minutes of critical thinking about the next seven days. This is the time to mentally review your immediate goals and decide what *deserves* your attention. You can do this by answering five basic questions:

1. What are my personal obligations?
2. What are my priority projects?
3. How much time do I have?
4. What are the next actions on my Todoist project lists?

5. Is there any item on my Someday/Maybe list that I'd like to focus on this week?

Your responses to these questions are extremely important because they will determine the amount of time you can devote to your goals during the next seven days.

The lesson here is that you *shouldn't* schedule your week with hundreds of activities, which is the quickest path to that feeling of overwhelm. Instead, it's better to recognize, ahead of time, a realistic amount of time that can be dedicated to your tasks.

Action #2: Apply the 80/20 Rule to Your Schedule

The 80/20 Rule, originally mentioned by Italian economist Vilfredo Pareto, says that 80% of your results often come from 20% of your efforts. So only a handful of your tasks will produce any sort of measurable result.

This rule can be applied to *any* industry or business. For example, 80% of revenue is generated by 20% of the salespeople; 80% of complaints come from only 20% of customers; and 80% of highway traffic is funneled through 20% of the roads.

My point here is that no matter what tasks and obligations you need to do weekly, there will *always* be a handful that produce extraordinary results. A few strategies will work well, while everything else will be a waste of your time.

You can apply this to your to-do list by *only* structuring your schedule where you focus on just the actions that generate a significant result and proactively ignore almost everything else.

During a weekly review, take a few minutes to carefully consider the answers to these questions:

- » What tasks are causing 80% of my problems and unhappiness?

- » What core activities have the biggest impact on my career?

- » What experiences produce 80% of my fulfillment and happiness?

- » Who are the people that cause 80% of my enjoyment and make me feel truly engaged?

- » Who are the 20% of people who cause me to feel angry, unhappy, and unfulfilled?

- » What habits make up 80% of my efficiency or effectiveness?

You don't have to ask all these questions every week. But they should always be in the back of your mind when you're doing a weekly review. If you get busy, you can simplify everything by asking one simple question: "Does this task help or hinder my ability to work on one of my five goals?"

Be honest with yourself here. Your time is a finite resource. Every minute spent on a time-wasting activity is one less minute that you have for your goals. If you feel something takes away time from those crucial goals, then avoid doing it at *all* costs.

Remember: Never let other people's priorities become your own.

Action #3: Block Out Time on a Calendar

After identifying those 80/20 tasks, it's time to put these activities into your calendar.

To get started, I recommend five simple actions:

1. **Begin by blocking out time for the commitments that you already have that involve other people or deadlines.** These are meetings, appointments, and previously scheduled events. There is no flexibility for these commitments, so they should be the first items to put on your calendar.

2. **Block out time for the tasks that are high priorities as well as those that require greater concentration.** You can make time for them by looking at your project lists, identifying the actions that need to be completed next, and scheduling time to work on these activities. If you don't make time for these activities, you'll end up focusing on the tasks that don't have as much of a positive impact on your life.

3. **Practice batching and create theme days.** One way to structure your time is to focus on one type of activity for an extended block of time. This is often called *batching tasks*. The benefit of batching is that you remove the stress that often comes from having too many tasks on your to-do list. Instead of trying to tackle everything on one day, you set aside time each week to singularly focus on similar tasks.

   For instance, you can batch activities like responding to email, posting on social media, returning phone calls, going to appointments, and handling administrative tasks. These can be done in blocks throughout the day. Any task that you regularly do can be batched with similar tasks.

4. **Block out time for personal hobbies, such as reading or going to listen to a speaker talk on a topic that is interesting to you.** You may also find it helpful to block out time to spend with your children doing homework or getting ready for bed. You should also block out time to have a date night with your spouse. It doesn't have to be anything fancy or expensive; just spending the time together to build a healthy relationship will be beneficial to your overall well-being.

5. **Set aside "flexible time" for unexpected tasks and issues that require your immediate attention.** By leaving parts of your calendar open, you can take care of these issues without derailing your plans to work on the important stuff.

If you want to see an example of what my weekly schedule looks like, check out the visual walkthrough that I provide on the free companion website.

Step #3: Build the "Todoist Daily Review" Habit

This final step requires you to build a habit. At the beginning of every day (or the night before), set aside 5 to 10 minutes to briefly review all the tasks you have scheduled in Todoist.

This review habit is important because it helps you reinforce the day's priorities, recognize any potential last-minute conflicts, and identify the most important tasks related to your goals.

During this review session, you should think carefully about the answers to these key questions:

- » What appointments and meetings require me to be somewhere at a set time?

- » Are there any emergency emails that need to be addressed immediately?

- » What are the tasks related to my time blocks that I need to complete?

- » Is there an appointment or activity that might take longer than expected? Could this negatively impact my schedule?

- » What are the 80/20 tasks that will have the biggest impact on my long-term success?

- » How does each task relate to my goals?

- » What is the hardest, most challenging task that I'm dreading? Should I work on this task before anything else?

This review habit is critical because it provides structure for each day. When you constantly force yourself to identify what's important, you'll discover that the bulk of your time is spent on the actions that truly matter in your personal and professional life.

Well, that's it for all the core strategies to use with Todoist. Now, let me talk about one last thing before we close out the book—advanced hacks you can use to combine Todoist with other popular apps and online tools.

23 Advanced Strategies to Maximize Your Todoist Experience

There are many advanced features you can use to maximize your experience with Todoist. A few of them are offered by the good folks at Todoist, but most can be found as recipes on IFTTT.com.

You probably don't *need* to use many of these advanced features. They are just options. But if you'd like to save time or make your life a little bit easier, then the following 23 strategies can be invaluable. On the other hand, if you've never even heard of an application that I mention, then feel free to skip past the suggestion.

We'll start with a few strategies provided by Todoist, then I'll dive into the recipes that you can find on IFTTT.

#1. Add browser plugins. A browser plugin is a simple applet that runs on top of your favorite browser, such as Google Chrome or Firefox. These can be great for generating tasks in Todoist, while viewing a webpage. With a few clicks, you can turn the URL into a task that you can work on later. To get started, visit Todoist's homepage and click the link for Chrome, Firefox, or Safari.

#2. Add an email plugin. This strategy can be a huge time-saver if you're someone who schedules a lot of tasks from email. Having a single button email plugin makes it turn any message into a task or an appointment on your calendar. Todoist offers special plugins for both Outlook and Gmail.

#3. Create recurring tasks based on completion date. The typical way to create recurring tasks based upon a specific start date is to use the "starting" modifier. For example, if you have a task that is, "every two weeks starting August 1" you will create a task for August 1 that will recur on August 15 then August 29 then September 12, and so on. This is basic stuff that we've already covered.

An advanced way to create a recurring task is to use a "not" symbol in your modifier, which is: *!*

For instance, you could create a task like: *every! two weeks starting August 1*

What this does is change the next recurring dates to **two weeks after the completion date** rather than two weeks after the task starts.

If you add the task on August 1 but don't complete it until August 3, then the next time you will see this task will be on August 17, not August 15. This can be extremely useful in situations where the exact date matters less than simply remembering to do an activity on a regular basis. For example, I use this feature for recurring personal chores like getting a haircut, mowing the lawn, and going grocery shopping.

#4. Integrate with Google Drive and Dropbox (premium). Todoist premium users have an endless ability to add comments to their tasks. When you tap or click the Comment button on a task, you can then add notes or upload a multimedia file. Unfortunately, there is a limit on the file size of any item that's added to a task—right now it's 20 MB per task.

You can get around this limit by linking your Google Drive and/or Dropbox accounts with Todoist. All you have to do is copy a link of a file (or folder) from one of these services, and then add the link as a comment to a specific task.

#5. Use Todoist on your Apple Watch. Yes, your tasks can even be accessed on your Apple Watch—all you need to do is update the latest

Todoist iOS for this wearable device. Then you're free to add, edit, and complete tasks while on the go using your Apple Watch.

#6. Use Todoist on your Android Wear. The reasons you'd use Todoist with Android Wear are the same as with your Apple Watch. The difference is how you'd create a task.

For instance, when using Android Wear, simply speak, "Okay, Google, start to-do list," and speak the name of the task. You can create due dates by using natural language like, "every two weeks starting today." These tasks will instantly appear in your Todoist Inbox.

#7. Create a Trello card every time you create a new task. Trello is a collaboration tool that organizes your projects into boards. It's great for telling you what's being worked on, who's working on it, and what tasks need to be completed in a project.

This is a straightforward strategy: whenever you add a task in Todoist, the IFTTT recipe will automatically create a card in Trello. Here is the link to the IFTTT recipe.

#8. Trello tasks assigned to me go into Todoist. This strategy is the reverse of the one I just described. Whenever someone creates a card in Trello and tags you, a task will be created automatically in Todoist. Here is the link to the IFTTT recipe.

#9. Create a task when you star an email in Gmail. Earlier in this section, we talked about how you could create tasks from Gmail with an applet button. But maybe you often forget to add tasks when you're going through your messages. So with this recipe, you can create a new task whenever you *star* an email, which is a tool that Gmail uses to identify messages as being important. Here is the link to the IFTTT recipe.

#10. Create a copy of all tasks you complete in a Gmail message. Maybe you have a boss or coworker that needs to know what you are doing. This recipe will generate a summary of tasks you've completed into a Gmail message that can be delivered to anyone that you designate. Here is the link to the IFTTT recipe.

#11. Put completed tasks into Google Sheets. If you're someone who likes to keep track of everything, then this recipe can save you a lot of time. One of the best places to keep information is the Google Sheets program. With this recipe, whenever you complete a task in Todoist, it's automatically put into a spreadsheet that you designate. This is a great way to get a complete picture of what you're accomplishing on a daily basis. Here is the link to the IFTTT recipe.

#12. Automatically turn Google Calendar events into tasks. As I mentioned in the previous section, syncing Google Calendar with Todoist allows you to see all your tasks and appointments in a single interface. So with this recipe, you can turn any event that goes on your calendar into tasks. Here is the link to the IFTTT recipe.

#13. Automatically create a Google Calendar event for new Todoist tasks. You can also reverse the previous strategy and create a calendar event for every task that you create. A word of warning: this can get pretty overwhelming if you're someone who is constantly adding tasks to your to-do list. Here is the link to the IFTTT recipe.

#14. Get a reminder to bring an umbrella if tomorrow's forecast says rain. This simple recipe can keep the rain off your head. You could even modify your existing IFTTT to let you know when sunny weather is expected so you could bike to work or exercise outdoors. With this simple strategy, there are a lot of options that help you take specific actions based on the weather. Here is the link to the IFTTT recipe.

#15. Add a reminder for missed phone calls. When you miss a phone call, a Todoist task will be created immediately to remind you to call this person back. Here is the link to the IFTTT recipe.

#16. Save new iOS reminders as a task. With this recipe, you can use the Siri function of the iOS platform to automatically create tasks into reminders This is perfect for those moments when you're on the move and literally can't type a message (like when driving or exercising). Here is the link to the IFTTT recipe.

#17. Add a Pocket reading list to Todoist. Pocket is an application that allows you to save interesting articles, blog posts, videos, and other types of multimedia content that you can view later. Once saved to Pocket, this content is available on any device where you have it installed—like your phone, tablet, or computer. So with this strategy, you can create a task in Todoist to go through a specific piece of content whenever it's saved to Pocket. Here is the link to the IFTTT recipe.

#18. Add a note in Evernote whenever you add a specific label in Todoist. As I've previously mentioned, Evernote allows users to create a "note" that can be a piece of formatted text, a full webpage or webpage excerpt, a photograph, a voice memo, or file attachment.

If you're someone who uses Evernote frequently, you can create an @evernote label, and then whenever you add that label to a task in Todoist, it will be archived in Evernote. Here is the link to the IFTTT recipe.

#19. Use SMS to remember specific tasks. This strategy will automatically create a Todoist task whenever someone sends you an SMS message with the words "remember to." This is useful if your spouse, significant other, or friend likes to remind you to complete errands or chores. Here is the link to the IFTTT recipe.

#20. Notify project members in Slack when a task is created. Slack is a team workflow application. It makes it easy to delegate, track, and communicate with team members of a specific project. It's the main tool that I personally use to communicate with my virtual assistant and team members. With this strategy, anyone who is attached as a collaborator in Todoist will get an automatic notification whenever you create a new task. Here is the link to the IFTTT recipe.

#21. Post to Slack once you've completed a task. If other team members are waiting on you to complete a task so they can start on an action, this strategy will send them an automatic notification. Here is the link to the IFTTT recipe.

#22. Memorialize completed tasks in Onenote. Microsoft OneNote is a free-form program that lets you gather notes (handwritten or typed), drawings, screen clippings, and audio commentaries all in one place. With this strategy, you can turn all your completed Todoist tasks into a single file that you review whenever you want. Here is the link to the IFTTT recipe.

#23. Create a task whenever you receive a priority email in Microsoft Office. If you use Office, this strategy can be a great time-saver. Most priority messages require you to take action on a specific project. With this strategy, a task will be created automatically whenever you receive one of these priority messages. Here is the link to the IFTTT recipe.

As you can see, there are many interesting hacks you can use to maximize your Todoist experience. If you'd like to learn more about these strategies (and check out others that I didn't include), then I recommend checking out the Todoist page on the IFTTT website.

Final Thoughts on Master Todoist

Todoist has changed my life. And after reading this book, I hope you've come to realize how this simple app can have an amazing impact on your time management efforts. No longer do you need to use multiple tools to run your life. Instead, you can use Todoist to capture all your open loops and be 100% confident that you won't miss an important task or appointment.

While I did my best to simplify all Todoist's available features, you still might not know how to get started with that app.

Don't worry if this sounds like you!

A great thing about Todoist is it's easy to use—even if you're not comfortable with technology.

You can download the app right now, then be up and running within the next five minutes.

That's why I recommend four simple steps for getting started.

First, if you haven't installed the app, then I urge you to do so right now. Again, here is a list of links to every platform that Todoist offers:

1. Web
2. Android Phone
3. Android Tablet
4. Android Wear
5. iPhone
6. iPad
7. Apple Watch
8. Windows

9. MacOS

10. Chrome

11. Firefox

12. Safari

13. Outlook

14. Gmail

Be sure to add this account on every single device that you use. That way, you'll always have your task management list in front of you, ready to go.

Next, I recommend creating a project for every major area of your life. If you get stuck, you can use the seven areas that most people focus on:

1. Career

2. Finance

3. Leisure

4. Health

5. Relationships

6. Service

7. Spirituality

Inside each of these parent projects, create subprojects for any action that requires multiple steps to complete. It's up to you what projects *you* create—just think of the major "buckets" in your life and add projects based on these recurring activities.

Third, make that commitment to review Todoist daily. Check off tasks you've completed. Add new ones that you'd like to accomplish. And create a project whenever you start a new multistep activity.

The one reason some people fail to get results with their to-do lists is they don't fully commit to the process. So if you take five minutes daily to open Todoist, then you'll eventually build a very powerful habit of reviewing your tasks. Once that happens, you'll be 100% confident that anything stored in this app will be there when you need it.

Finally, when you're comfortable with the core features of Todoist, you can incorporate some of the 23 advanced strategies I just mentioned. Go to IFTTT.com to automate the other apps and programs that you typically use, like Evernote, Slack, or Gmail. If you're someone who likes to systematize their life as much as possible, then these recipes can streamline many of the actions you do frequently.

Now it's your turn.

If used correctly, Todoist can become the central hub where you manage all your tasks, projects, and appointments. But it's only as useful as its user. I encourage you to take that first step and commit to using this app daily.

Don't be afraid to make mistakes—that's the best way to learn something. The more time you invest in the app, the more you will come to rely on it like millions of other users.

Good luck!

Steve "S.J." Scott

One Last Reminder ...

We've covered a wealth of information in this book, but there's a lot more you can learn about Todoist. In fact, I've created a small companion website that includes many resources mentioned throughout *Master Todoist*.

Here are just a few things I've included:

» A video walkthrough the major features—including Tasks, Projects, Labels, and the account features.

» A video walkthrough of the importing project feature.

» A list of all the links included in this book.

» A visual walkthrough of the time blocking technique that I use to schedule my week.

» Large-sized images of all the screenshots included in this book.

Plus, I will be adding more goodies to this website in the months to come. So, if you're interested in expanding on what you've learned in this book, then click this link and join us today:

www.developgoodhabits.com/todoist-website

Thank You!

Before you go, we'd like to say thank you for purchasing my book.

You could have picked from dozens of books on habit development, but you took a chance and checked out this one.

So, big thanks for downloading this book and reading all the way to the end.

Now we'd like ask for a small favor. **Could you please take a minute or two and leave a review for this book on Amazon?**

This feedback will help us continue to write the kind of Kindle books that help you get results. And if you loved it, please let us know.

More Books by Steve

» *The Anti-Procrastination Habit: A Simple Guide to Mastering Difficult Tasks*

» *10-Minute Mindfulness: 71 Habits for Living in the Present Moment*

» *Habit Stacking: 127 Small Changes to Improve Your Health, Wealth, and Happiness*

» *Novice to Expert: 6 Steps to Learn Anything, Increase Your Knowledge, and Master New Skills*

» *Declutter Your Mind: How to Stop Worrying, Relieve Anxiety, and Eliminate Negative Thinking*

» *The Miracle Morning for Writers: How to Build a Writing Ritual That Increases Your Impact and Your Income*

» *10-Minute Digital Declutter: The Simple Habit to Eliminate Technology Overload*

» *10-Minute Declutter: The Stress-Free Habit for Simplifying Your Home*

» *The Accountability Manifesto: How Accountability Helps You Stick to Goals*

» *Confident You: An Introvert's Guide to Success in Life and Business*

» *Exercise Every Day: 32 Tactics for Building the Exercise Habit (Even If You Hate Working Out)*

» *The Daily Entrepreneur: 33 Success Habits for Small Business Owners, Freelancers and Aspiring 9-to-5 Escape Artists*

» *Master Evernote: The Unofficial Guide to Organizing Your Life with Evernote (Plus 75 Ideas for Getting Started)*

» *Bad Habits No More: 25 Steps to Break Any Bad Habit*

» *To-Do List Makeover: A Simple Guide to Getting the Important Things Done*

» *23 Anti-Procrastination Habits: How to Stop Being Lazy and Get Results in Your Life*

» *S.M.A.R.T. Goals Made Simple: 10 Steps to Master Your Personal and Career Goals*

» *115 Productivity Apps to Maximize Your Time: Apps for iPhone, iPad, Android, Kindle Fire and PC/iOS Desktop Computers*

» *Writing Habit Mastery: How to Write 2,000 Words a Day and Forever Cure Writer's Block*

» *Daily Inbox Zero: 9 Proven Steps to Eliminate Email Overload*

» *Wake Up Successful: How to Increase Your Energy and Achieve Any Goal with a Morning Routine*

» *10,000 Steps Blueprint: The Daily Walking Habit for Healthy Weight Loss and Lifelong Fitness*

» *70 Healthy Habits: How to Eat Better, Feel Great, Get More Energy and Live a Healthy Lifestyle*

» *Resolutions That Stick! How 12 Habits Can Transform Your New Year*